DAUGHTER OF AFRICA

1998-99 NWMS READING BOOKS

RESOURCE BOOK FOR THE LEADER

IMAGINE THE HARVEST
Edited by Beverlee Borbe

FOR THE READER

AGAINST THE TIDE
The Miracle of Growth in the Netherlands
By Cisca Verwoerd

DAUGHTER OF AFRICA
The Story of Juliet Ndzimandze
By Charles Gailey

JUST CAUSE
How Nazarene Students Are Changing Their World
By Frank Moore

PLACES CALLED INDIA
By Tim Crutcher

PREACHER WITH A MISSION
The Story of Nina Griggs Gunter
By Helen Temple

WINDOWS TO ALBANIA
By Connie Griffith Patrick

BY CHUCK GAILEY

DAUGHTER OF AFRICA

THE STORY OF
JULIET NDZIMANDZE

Nazarene Publishing House
Kansas City, Missouri

Lovingly dedicated to
my wife, Doris.
She is my best friend and coworker,
and she saved the letters
that helped make this book possible.

Contents

Dr. Charles "Chuck" Gailey is director of the School of World Mission and Evangelism at Nazarene Theological Seminary, Kansas City, Missouri, where he is engaged in training new missionary candidates. Prior to this assignment, he and his wife, Doris, were missionaries to Swaziland for thirteen years.

Dr. Gailey is the author of numerous articles and reviews in publications such as *World Mission* and *Missiology* and is a well-known speaker who has spoken at conferences and retreats throughout the world.

Preface

Juliet Ndzimandze was a remarkable person. Her ministry originated in her home nation of Swaziland in Africa and spread to other parts of the globe, including Britain, the United States, Germany, and the Netherlands.

Juliet Ndzimandze was also our friend. We reveled in her preaching and rejoiced in her faithfulness. Her humor was legendary, and it was joined to remarkably good sense. She was such a strong leader that grown men were heard to say, "When we see Juliet, we tremble."

Waving the flag of Swaziland at Dr. Chapman's 100th birthday celebration, Temple City, California.

It is an honor to be asked to write her legacy. This book really represents a team effort with the church in Swaziland. Much of the research was done in Africa during the summer of 1996. I wish to extend grateful thanks to my wife, Doris, my cointerviewer; to the dozens of people who contributed through interviews and letters; and especially to Solomon Magagula, district superintendent of the Swaziland Central District, who had the invaluable foresight to have Juliet record her life story just months before her death.

May those who read this be as inspired and blessed as we have been in compiling the dramatic story of this evangelist to the world.

Prologue

Runners were dispatched across the green hills of northern Swaziland: "Schmelzenbach is dying!" The pioneer missionary had been warned not to go to the fever-ridden lowlands, but his vision of lost humanity there had sent him anyway. Repeated bouts with malaria had resulted in the dreaded blackwater fever. His breath was now coming in short, spasmodic gasps. Three days previous he had tried to get up to go with other missionaries farther north, but he had collapsed back into his bed. Now the end was near.

One of the most important persons the runners had to notify was Solomon Ndzimandze (zee-MAHN-zee). He had been the very first pastor that Harmon Schmelzenbach had appointed and was very close to Harmon in the ministry. They must get the word to him at once.

The out-of-breath runner climbed the forested mountain as he approached Helehele (hay-lee-HAY-lee), where the Ndzimandzes pastored. When he reached the church, he found that Solomon Ndzimandze himself was desperately ill. He was, in fact, too ill to preach, and his wife, Martha, was filling that role.

In this situation Martha knew she must respond. She hurried over the miles of mountain paths to say farewell to her missionary. Up and down, up and down, her feet fairly ran as the golden sleeves of the sun washed the mountain peaks.

In Martha's womb on that sad journey was a child, the last to be born to the family. Little did she realize on that late autumn morning that the child she was carrying would live to bless the earth. This baby would become a woman who would evangelize throughout Africa and then in the British Isles, the Netherlands, Germany, and America. She would be the first Nazarene woman to be ordained in Africa. She would associate with royalty and prime ministers. She would travel the world and see thousands come to know Jesus as Savior and Lord.

For in the very year that Harmon Schmelzenbach passed from this earth, a child was born who would carry the same passionate and heart-wrenching burden for the peoples of the globe. The last born in the home of the first African Nazarene pastor would become the first African woman to be an evangelist to the world.

1

Anaheim

THE BIG ARC LIGHTS SWIVELED along the rails 60 feet above the floor. The beams intersected and crisscrossed as the lighting of the great Anaheim Convention Center dimmed. The shining rays then dissolved into one great shaft of light that zeroed in on the podium. Six thousand people waited as a tall, slightly built woman from Africa rose to speak.

With typical good humor, she began, "This is my first time to attend a General Assembly, and I think it's going to be my last!" The audience roared.

After the laughter died down, she commented on the offering that had just been taken. "I noticed that Dr. Nees challenged us to give, and then he couldn't find his wallet!" The great Nazarene World Mission Society (NWMS) General Convention crowd laughed again. They could see that this was someone they were going to love. This was Juliet Ndzimandze, a preacher's daughter born in the obscure little mountain hamlet of Helehele in Swaziland.

But tonight, June 20, 1985, she was standing in Anaheim, California, before a capacity crowd. The

Crusader Choir from Northwest Nazarene College had just sung. She had been introduced by Dr. L. Guy Nees as a "daughter of Africa." Her prayer partners around the world were praying for her. She seized the moment.

Juliet spoke from Acts 16:6-10, about Paul's vision of the Macedonian who had called to him, "Come over . . . and help us." She reminded the crowd that others need to know about Jesus. At the height of the message she said,

> Christ came your way, Christ came my way, because someone sacrificed, someone prayed, someone gave. Someone gave so that missionaries could come my way. I am no longer the same. I have been transformed. I have been saved and sanctified. A Swazi woman has been set free indeed!

A great chorus of "Amens" resounded throughout the arena. She continued:

> Others need to hear the redemption story. Others need to be set free from utter darkness to walk in God's light. We need to do something about this message!

> We pride ourselves on being among the top 10 missionary-sending organizations. We have 609 missionaries. We are really doing well. Thirty-six colleges overseas—we are a marvelous group, really. We are in 75 countries. We have done well, don't you think?

> Nazarenes, I challenge you today. Seventy-five countries are too few for our Father! Lift up your eyes! Look around! The fields are

Speaking at the Anaheim Convention Center (1985 General Assembly).

ready for harvest. We need not just vision but *extraordinary* vision. The end is not yet! Go forward in the power of the Holy Spirit! God is with us!

Even today a tear may come to one's eyes while listening to the tape recording of Juliet's impassioned plea. Her impact on the United States was not limited to the NWMS General Convention. After the convention she traveled across the United States for three months, and remarkable blessing ensued. At one district assembly the general superintendent couldn't make it, so they asked her to fill in. She agreed but said, "I know that I'm going in where I shouldn't be—and I won't forget that." Needless to say, she did well.

Juliet's tour of the South Carolina District was

a highlight of her American trip. Revival broke out as people sought the Lord. Some of the people in South Carolina who heard her corresponded with her for the rest of her life. Her simple response to the way God had used her was "I praise His name."

There were the customary faux pas, of course. When introduced to a young lady from Las Vegas, Nevada, she replied, "Oh, that wicked city?" The young lady gasped in shock, and Juliet was quickly assured that there were some good people who lived there.

To some other friends she commented, "Americans are funny people. They drive their cars into their houses and have a pig under the sink to eat the garbage!"

Everywhere she went, Juliet endeared herself to people. Anaheim may have been the first time this "daughter of Africa" ministered in America, but it would most certainly not be the last.

2

Daughter of Her Father

THE DEMENTED MAN staggered up the path leading to the church building. His haphazard mutterings seemed to match the jerking of his body. His eyes rolled backward into their sockets. A trace of saliva appeared at the corner of his mouth as his swaying body came closer to the church.

The appearance of a mentally disadvantaged person at the Helehele church was not that uncommon. This congregation had become known all over northern Swaziland as a place where the physically and mentally ill could come and be prayed for. What was different on this spring morning was that the grown-ups were all away. Of all the parsonage family, only six-year-old Juliet was there.

Juliet observed the man careening uncertainly through the gate. What should she do? Her father would pray for the man, but he was not here. She was the daughter of her father—she had to do something to help this poor man. In a flash, a plan of action materialized. She couldn't read, but she could sing.

Juliet called for her three-year-old friend Patricia and said to her, "We must sing to this man." The two little girls began to sing "I Will Make the Darkness Light Before You." They merely stood before the man and sang.

Juliet noticed that the man seemed surprised at first by the sight of these two very small children. She didn't know what else to do, so she and her young friend sang the same verses again: "If you walk by the way, I will lead you . . ."

Juliet then noticed that the jerking of the man's body had diminished. They kept singing: "With an everlasting love I'll love you . . ." His mutterings quieted some. They kept singing still, over and over: "What is wrong I'll make it right before you . . ."

Amazingly, the rolling eyes began to drop and finally focused as the man regained his senses. The darkness was made light before him. Years later Juliet would remember this day as her earliest excursion into ministry. Her father was a minister, and she was the daughter of her father.

Juliet Kayise (ky-YEE-seh) Ndzimandze was born on Christmas Day 1929. She grew up with the rich heritage of a Nazarene parsonage family. Although it was highly unusual in those days for a Swazi man to be seen holding an infant, her father often carried Juliet in his arms. The church people began to call her Intombi Kayise (in-tome-bee ky-YEE-seh), or Kayise for short, which means "daughter of her father." The name stuck. In later life, Juliet said (as in the story of Joseph), "My father loved me more than all the children in the home."

Juliet's father, Solomon Ndzimandze, was the

first Nazarene pastor in Africa, and he was in the first group to be ordained. His wife, Martha, was a good preacher in her own right, and she was so revered by the church that in later years the church newspaper referred to her as "our mother in Israel." Together, Solomon and Martha formed a model Christian home.

On the day that Solomon himself was born, his parents' home burned to the ground. Because of the incident, his parents named him Malangabi (ma-lan-GAH-bee), which means "flames." Rev. Ndzi-mandze liked his name very much. He often said that God knew what his work would be—that he was going to be a flame for the gospel.

After Solomon's conversion, his pastor gave him two instructions: "You should pray always, and you should always give an offering." Solomon accepted these instructions, and they became the hallmarks of his life, both in ministry and in the home.

Solomon went to pray in his church building every evening from 5 till 7. When Juliet was a child, Solomon would take her with him every day. Through these times the father and daughter grew very close. As an adult, Juliet chose the same time of day to pray "because that is when my father prayed." Indeed, she was the daughter of her father in prayer. "Train up a child in the way he should go: and when he is old, he will not depart from it" (Prov. 22:6, KJV).

In the dirt floor of the church at Helehele, there was a depression where Solomon prayed. At times during the quarterly meeting of pastors, some pastors would fall asleep. When asked why they were so tired, they would reply, "Solomon kept us up praying last night." In later years, Bible college students remembered being awakened at night by the burdened prayers of Juliet.

Solomon also had a keen sense of humor. At the church Christmas feast, many people from the community would come who never entered the church at any other time of the year. Solomon knew that they were there just to get food, so before eating he would say, "Let us pray." And he would pray—and pray—and pray an extremely long prayer. Afterward he would laugh heartily, saying he knew he was tempting them with the delicious aromas wafting through the air. He loved to laugh.

Like her father, Juliet had a great sense of humor. She loved to play practical jokes on missionaries and other friends, and then she would erupt into laughter so heartily the tears would come. Once on a Saturday night soon after some new missionaries had arrived, a disoriented drunk sat down, muttering, right outside their bedroom window. It was a harmless situation, but the new missionaries were scared to death. The next Saturday night the missionaries were in the kitchen. Suddenly there was a loud muttering again outside. But when they looked out the window, it was Juliet, laughing so hard she could hardly stand up!

Solomon Ndzimandze liked nice clothes. Juliet did too. For her, it was elegance on a budget. She always looked as though she had stepped right out of a dress shop. Sometimes she felt she had to look after the missionaries in this regard. Missionary Della Boggs usually wore everyday shoes as she traveled the muddy paths to and from class. When Juliet heard that Della's sister was coming for a visit from the United States, she said to Della, "Now don't embarrass us. You must wear your best shoes while your sister is here."

Solomon Ndzimandze was a sacrificial giver. Juliet was 22 years old when she saw a missionary open her father's Alabaster box. Out tumbled $15. By this time the elder Ndzimandze was both retired and blind and was receiving only $5 a month to support his family. Juliet said, "My heart was greatly touched. I vowed that I too would share in this giving of love to my Savior. I promised to give a second tithe to Him in my Alabaster box. In times of special blessing I have put in even more than this."

If Juliet's parents ever hurt anyone with their words, they quickly apologized. Kind words were the rule in the home. Juliet's close friend Ellen said, "I never heard her speak harshly to anyone."

Petrus Pato, a Swazi pastor and longtime colleague of Juliet, said, "Juliet's father was a giant— he was so strong. And Juliet got many characteristics from her father." District Superintendent Solomon Magagula recalled that "Solomon Ndzimandze was a person of prayer, one who liked clothes, and one who liked to laugh." Juliet was a daughter of her father indeed.

In his later life, Solomon Ndzimandze became

very ill. One day he called all of his family to his bedside. With great effort, he rose up slightly in bed, raised one arm, and lifted up the Bible in his hand. Emotion nearly choked his words as he asked his children, "Who will carry this Book?" The older brothers just sat there. But Juliet, even though young, got up and went to her father. She took the Bible and said, "I will carry the Book." She was truly a daughter of her father—not only of her earthly father but her Heavenly Father as well.

3

Child of God

JULIET ENTERED SCHOOL at six years of age and stayed in the local school until completing standard four (grade six), which was the highest level offered. Even her early teachers recognized her as a bright student. She then went to boarding school at Endzingeni for standards five and six. It was a difficult experience for Juliet, being so young and so far away from home for a large part of the year. There were lonely times when she wished she could be back on the green mountain at Helehele, but she persevered.

During these times at boarding school, Juliet did more than just study. Although she had not yet become a Christian, she remembered that her parents were people of prayer, and she began to pray at the same hour in the evenings as she knew they were faithfully doing.

In 1943 an evangelist from Zululand, Rev. Bhengu, came to conduct services at Endzingeni, and a great revival ensued. It affected everyone in the school and church, and Juliet was saved. But the evangelist moved on, revival fires cooled, and so did Juliet's religious experience. Shortly thereafter she left for high school at Manzini.

In the early weeks of her final year of high school, the school arranged revival services for young people. They began at 4 P.M., after the school day was concluded. Restless youngsters, tired after a long day of lessons, shuffled into the meeting. They were not very responsive, and resistance was the order of the day. In fact, some of the graduating seniors said, "We will never go to the altar." All week there had been virtually no response. Finally Friday arrived.

Juliet later testified that, as the final service began, "God spoke to me forcefully. I was to make a choice, as Moses made a choice. God continued to speak with me during the sermon. When the invitation was made, not minding my friends, I rushed to the altar." Many others followed her, and Juliet always believed that her obedience, even in the face of peer pressure, was a key that helped others find the Lord.

Juliet's struggle did not end once she found the altar. The leaders encouraged fellow Christians to help those who were drawn to the altar. People came to pray and counsel with everyone except Juliet. She was left alone.

After a time, however, Juliet heard someone come and kneel down beside her. It was the missionary medical doctor David Hynd, who had left his work at the hospital. Even though he had been very busy, he had decided to drop by the church and see what was happening in the teen revival service. As he prayed with Juliet, he recited, "If we confess our sins, he is faithful and just to forgive us our sins, and to cleanse us from all unrighteous-ness" (1 John 1:9, KJV).

That was the encouragement Juliet needed. She said, "I confess my sins. I choose Jesus today." Then she felt the burden lift. She was forgiven, and she had peace in her heart. Later that year she was sanctified. From that time forward she held on to her newfound faith. Although she was criticized and ridiculed by her peers, she determined to fol-low Jesus, even if she had to walk alone. And that day was not far off.

All through her senior year, Juliet thought she would prepare for a career in nursing. She was one of the most highly educated young persons of her day. In those days there was no higher level course for nurses in Swaziland, so Juliet began prepara-tions to go to Johannesburg, South Africa, for her nurse's training. Arrangements were made for her application, and the necessary forms were filled out. A friend of her father agreed to accompany her. It seemed everything was in order for her fu-ture career.

Two weeks before Juliet was to leave for Johan-nesburg, students from the Nazarene Bible College at Siteki came to her church to conduct a Sunday morning service. While the students were speaking and testifying, suddenly, almost like an audible voice, came an impression in her heart: "God wants you."

Like many young people of every generation, Juliet tried to reason with God. As she clenched her fists, she said to Him, "But I have done all of this studying." When that didn't work, she said, "My parents need my help." When God didn't respond to that, she said, "My sister is sick." When God remained silent, she said, "My father is sick." When there was still no response, she said, "If I earn a nurse's salary, I'll be able to help my parents." Still the call came. All her arguments had fallen flat as a pancake before God. By this time the invitation was being given.

"Would all who feel a call from God please come forward?" For the rest of her days Juliet never knew how she made her way to the altar. But suddenly there she was, and it was there, through blinding tears, that she agreed to the call of God.

Then the battle royal began.

4

"Foolish Girl!"

YOU'RE CRAZY!" The taunt was thrown carelessly across the schoolyard. It was the typical reaction of Juliet's peers when they heard that she was going to attend Bible college. It hurt to hear people say such things, but even Juliet had to wonder if there was validity in what they were saying.

There was no course of study at the Nazarene Bible College in Siteki at that time for someone of Juliet's educational attainment. What would she study? She was so slow of speech that it was like an impediment. Her halting speech was downright painful, and her words came so slowly that people complained, "She takes too long." Others pronounced her too young, and still others said that there was no work for her to do. Some alleged, "She'll be a temptation to other students." Many commented, "She won't do a thing." People pointed fingers at her and said, "Foolish girl!"

Several missionary ladies saw the battle that Juliet was engaged in, and they called her to come to their home so they could pray for her. There in that home Juliet settled her call forever. That day she prayed, "Lord, because of Your cross, I am willing to be a fool." From that commitment she never turned back.

So it was, on a warm day in late summer, Juliet arrived on the campus of the Nazarene Bible College at Siteki. Many were still not convinced that it was the place for this very young, well-educated girl, but she had made her decision. While others were saying things like "Foolish girl!" God was whispering, "I will hold your hand."

The Bible college taught Juliet many things. One of the great lessons she learned was humility. Years later she testified, "God taught me to be humble, even though I was more highly educated than the other students." She continued, "The thing that really helped me was to learn how to pray."

There was a prayer house at Siteki for the students, and Juliet began to go there every day at 5 P.M., the time she knew her mother would be praying. This practice was a great help to her and had great ramifications for the future. Today people all over the continent of Africa remark on their memories of passing by the prayer house and hearing Juliet's voice lifted heavenward. Anyone who has ever resided on the Nazarene Bible College campus in Siteki knows about the hours Juliet spent in that little house dedicated as a place of prayer.

Juliet also soon gained practical skills in ministry. She and her friend Salome Dlamini faithfully taught a wayside Sunday School a mile or so from the Bible college. Many repented and believed in the Lord. An elderly lady in whose house Juliet had taught said in 1996, "She was always the same. I can't remember any bad thing about her life from then until the day that she died."

Nevertheless, when Juliet graduated from Bible college, there was still the question of what she would do. What happens to someone who doesn't fit the mold? The District Advisory Board customarily interviewed each student before he or she graduated, and it was the board's responsibility to appoint students to churches. When it came Juliet's turn, she walked in and sat down. She looked so young! The chair of the board said, "What is your calling?"

Juliet replied, "I don't know, but I know God has called me to preach."

Someone asked, "Will you be able to pastor a church?"

Juliet responded, "I don't know, but through God's help I will try." The answers were so weak they brought questions again. Was she a "foolish girl"?

After she had left and the door had been closed, the board decided to ask her to interpret for missionaries who needed it while teaching at the Bible college and to translate instructional materials. Years later someone said, "She was so young the board didn't know what to do with her, so they gave her something she couldn't do any harm with!"

Assisting the missionaries with course materials and instruction provided the perfect platform for more learning. She also studied correspondence courses from England. Occasionally she was given an opportunity to teach.

The principal, Ken Bedwell, recognized Juliet's

qualities and gifts and eventually gave her a full-time teaching position, the first national to be so honored. For the next 20 years Juliet was a successful and well-loved college instructor. Margaret Bedwell, at 87 years of age, remembers her as "our best teacher. All you can say about her is that she was a woman of faith, prayer, and obedience to God's will. She obeyed Him in all things."

Excellence was Juliet's theme. One African colleague said, "I observed her spending hours preparing for one class. She was so faithful!" Gradually, as she lectured more and more, her speech techniques improved. As with many who have overcome speech difficulties (such as Dwight L. Moody and Paul Cunningham), her speech actually became clearer and more precise than that of the average speaker. Eventually she began to delight not only her classes but also the church at large.

As Juliet's reputation grew, students were thrilled to have her for a teacher. One student said, "She taught so well. She didn't rush—she let it sink in." She continued to be known as a woman of prayer. Another student exclaimed, "The Spirit of God was all over the place as Juliet and others prayed all the time!" One former student reported, "The Bible college had revival because of her. We were revived by means of her life. She was in prayer at all times."

Two young sisters heard her speak at the Nomahasha Church. They talked together and agreed, "When we grow up, we want to be like this beautiful lady." One sister is an ordained elder today.

Students also appreciated Juliet's sense of humor. One young man on the verge of graduation was still single. Using a Swazi idiom referring to a young man's marriage prospects, Juliet asked him, "Did you buy pots for cooking?"

He replied, "No, I'll be eating popcorn," meaning that he would be staying alone. They laughed together, but this man, now a district superintendent, said, "I knew she was praying for me."

Not only was the spiritual tide high on campus, but also the educational level was steadily rising as well from that of a three-year program to a four-year program and finally to one leading to a degree. In addition, God was bringing to the campus students from a variety of African nations, including South Africa, Zambia, Malawi, and Mozambique. These individuals would return home and become significant contacts for Juliet during the next phase of her ministry.

Despite the prophets of doom, the Nazarene Bible College turned out to be a wonderful experience for Juliet. In fact, it became her home for 26 years. This "foolish girl" had become one of its most distinguished teachers and an honored alumna, but even greater things lay ahead.

Juliet had been willing to pray, "Lord, because of Your cross, I am willing to be a fool." Foolish girl? Indeed not! As Jim Elliot said, "He is no fool who gives what he cannot keep to gain what he cannot lose."

5

Prayer

G OODWIN, WHERE IS THAT RECEIPT?"
       "I don't know, Ms. Juliet. I think it's lost."
"Well, then, let us stop and pray."

Goodwin Chirwa would think to himself, "How can prayer help us find these things?" But after prayer, a miracle would happen. One of them would go straight to the place or book and find the missing item. Chirwa says today, "I can't explain how it happened—it just worked."

The most dominant single characteristic of the life of Juliet Ndzimandze was prayer. She was a person of prayer; it was her hallmark. She spent at least one and a half hours in prayer every day; often it was much more. She prayed for revival. She prayed for the college students. She prayed for pastors and district superintendents and missionaries. She prayed for the nations of the world.

Sometimes she would pray almost the entire day. Her friend Lucy said, "She could start in the morning and forget where she was—that was her life." Her district superintendent said after her passing, "She didn't just pray for a request for a few days. She would go on for two years or more."

Juliet was heavily burdened to pray for revival. A pastor remarked, "She prayed fervently without ceasing." She used to say to other Christians, "People are eating, but we must pray and fast. Pay the price! Pay the price!" Her pastor said, "Once I asked people to pray for revival individually at home. She reminded me that we must pray together as a church. We must pray, pray, pray for revival!" She was a living example of this scriptural principle. When she preached at revival services, people would flock to the altar. As one colleague put it, "It was as though the people were just waiting for the invitation. They would almost run to the altar."

It wasn't just the corporate body she prayed for. She prayed for individual needs and then waited patiently for the answers. Each year, even after leaving the Bible college, she would ask the registrar for a list of current students and teachers so that she could pray for each one by name every day. She continued this practice through the final semester of her life. When she was teaching, she urged her students to pray. Her formula for preparing a sermon was (1) pray until you get a burden, (2) pray until you get a scripture, (3) pray until you get the message.

A fellow teacher recounts, "She went to the prayer house to pray both during the day and the evening. That was her life, what she was known for." When the author served as principal of the Bible college and returned to the office late in the evening, he would hear her voice lifted in prayer in the prayer house. When she preached in Malawi in

The prayer house at the Swaziland Bible College.

1983, Pauline Kamanga was her interpreter. Mrs. Kamanga, who currently serves as head of World Relief in Malawi, recalls, "We shared a room for a week. I heard her praying, starting at 4 A.M. until 6 A.M. She prayed for people by name. I was so blessed. We were all blessed. She really knew how to pray." During one of Juliet's visits to the United States, her hostess reported refreshing times of prayer with Juliet. Later, after they had retired, she would hear Juliet still praying in her room.

All of this prayer did not mean that Juliet was a pie-in-the-sky Christian. Refreshingly, she had a great deal of common sense. When she was leading the service, she would not put up with nonsense. She cautioned people about long testimonies. She would say, "Are you going to take all day? Are you going to solve the problems of the world?" That's not to say that her own track record was perfect. During one period of her life she didn't realize how loudly she was praying in the night until she discovered that her student neighbors couldn't sleep!

One amazing example of the many answers to prayer Juliet received in her life is the story of the "miracle house" on Dlamini Street. When she accepted God's call into full-time evangelism in 1970, Juliet knew that she was giving up not only her position but also her accommodation. The Bible college administrators had been very kind to her and had offered her a room to stay in at the college in the town of Siteki. She knew, however, that without being on staff, she really had no claim to college housing. What should she do?

True to her life pattern, Juliet began to pray about this need. She asked her prayer partners to pray as well. About this time, the mayor of the nearby town of Manzini, who was also a Nazarene lay pastor, heard of her plight. He began to talk to Juliet about a new housing project. The town was building houses to sell for E10,000 (about U.S.$15,000). "Can we save you a building lot?" the mayor asked. To actually have a house of her own was almost unthinkable, because Juliet had no money. She knew she would have to decline, but she continued to pray.

The miracle house on Dlamini Street

The next time that the mayor saw her, though, he said, "We've saved a lot for you." Her prayer partners were praying. Over the next year, houses were built by the town on the vacant lots. Each time the mayor saw Juliet, he said, "We're saving a house for you." It all seemed so ridiculous—she didn't have the money! But she continually sought the Lord's will as to where she should live.

Time now was growing short. If she didn't buy a house in the housing project, it would be assigned to someone else. More prayers.

One day Juliet received a letter from a bank manager. It read, "Please sign the enclosed forms and bring them to the bank. Someone in Britain has sent you E10,000. You may come to the bank to pick up the money." A missionary who had been a teaching colleague had left her inheritance to Juliet. It was almost the exact amount needed for the house—and just in the nick of time! The "miracle house" was purchased.

The town of Manzini is the transportation hub of Swaziland. Having a home there enabled Juliet to travel more efficiently to her evangelistic assignments, and her home became a "hospitality center" where lady pastors and missionaries were welcome to stay. A friend said, "I never visited her without finding other visitors there."

Obtaining this miracle house strengthened Juliet's faith, and she used the story to strengthen the faith of others, telling it throughout Africa. In 1996, 10 years after he heard the story, a district superintendent in Central Africa could repeat it almost word for word.

Juliet tended to gather around her a group of others who had a God-given burden for prayer. Such a group was formally founded in northern Swaziland in 1970. For the past 27 years these prayer partners have met for several days each year to fast and pray. It has become known as Luketane Lwenthantazo (loo-keh-TAH-nee lwehn-tan-DAH-zoe), "the prayer chain." Early on, Juliet became the leader and would organize and call the meetings. They claimed the promise found in Isa. 62:6-7: "I have posted watchmen on your walls, O Jerusalem; they will never be silent day or night. You who call on the LORD, give yourselves no rest, and give him no rest till he establishes Jerusalem and makes her the praise of the earth."

The main topics of prayer for the group were the nation of Swaziland, young people, the schools, and revival in the churches. Juliet would also give each prayer partner a list of places where she would be preaching. They had special prayer for her when she traveled internationally. When in the United States she would say with confidence, "I know my prayer partners are in prayer for me." Great things happened when these partners met together.

At the beginning of one year the group met at Helehele, Juliet's birthplace. God's presence fell upon the group. People were on their knees crying out to God for three to four hours.

On another occasion there was a great drought throughout Swaziland. It seemed as though the clouds had dried up, and the food supply was in danger. People were desperate. The prayer chain met at the church at Black Mbuluzi ([m]boo-LOO-zee) and fasted and prayed. Around noontime God came in a mighty visitation upon the group. The group was "lost in wonder, love, and praise" (Charles Wesley). After they went to bed, they began to hear distant thunder, and around midnight the rain began to pour down upon the parched ground.

Juliet believed in fasting. Since Juliet was diabetic, missionary nurse Juanita Moon became concerned about her extended fasting. When she expressed to Juliet this concern about her health, Juliet replied, "You don't realize the strength I receive through fasting."

In 1986 a great visitation came upon a women's meeting at Siteki. Rev. Simon Mahlalela (ma-hla-LAY-lah) said, "I saw her face, which looked like snow. Great blessing came upon the meeting. Prayer has power!"

A missionary colleague said of Juliet, "It is inspiring to learn more and more of such a consistent, Spirit-filled life backed by unbelievable hours spent in prayer for individuals, the church, and all the nations of the world."

When Juliet Ndzimandze was around, she inspired not only the students and colleagues but the missionaries as well.

6

God's Ongoing Work

THOUGH JULIET'S EARLY SLOWNESS of speech was sometimes appreciated by the students, who thus had extra time to take notes, and by missionaries, who could easily hear what was being said in a second language, it was too halting and slow for public speaking. Juliet herself said, "In those days people did not like me to speak. They said I would take too long."

Once, the church sent her and Petrus Pato to a competition at Matsapha National High School to debate the reality of Christianity. When Juliet stood up, she dragged her words, and the students began to snicker. "Oh, poor girl," they said. "Why did they send you here to make you a laughingstock?" By the time she finished, however, one could hear a pin drop. They said, "This girl is so good she's dangerous!"

Gradually, however, Juliet's speaking skills improved, and it was not long until she became a wonderful speaker. In the mid-'60s, an offer came to Juliet to pastor the Magugu (mah-GOO-goo) Church of the Nazarene, located just a few miles away from the Bible college. She could continue her teaching in the college and pastor at the same time. She accepted the assignment and stayed for five years. This warmhearted and friendly church became a congenial setting for her to hone her preaching skills. She loved the people, and they loved her and listened attentively.

About this time, Juliet started receiving invitations to speak at young people's meetings. As her speaking improved, the door opened wider. Calls came for preaching in revivals, zone camps, and retreats. Churches from farther and farther away were calling her. Evangelism was gradually becoming a significant part of her ministry.

In 1966 two significant events occurred. The first was that Juliet was elected president of the Nazarene Young People's Society (NYPS—now NYI, Nazarene Youth International) for all of Swaziland. She had already been active in NYPS activities, both as a local president and in zone work. Nevertheless, she was surprised to be elected. It had always been men elected to this post. To this day, Juliet is the only woman in the history of Swaziland to have held this position.

Juliet did a tremendous job in her new role. Increases in every area took place under her leadership. Membership grew, programs were revitalized, and a singing group toured the nation. A flood of literature directed toward youth appeared in the district paper, *Umphaphamisi* (um-pah-pah-MEE-see). Juliet wrote many articles herself. One of her favorite themes was the great debt she owed. Her articles had titles like "Young people! We have a great debt! How will we pay it?" Her message in the October—December 1968 issue of *Umphaphamisi* was typical: "I am on fire! I can't sleep either day or night; I am disturbed by the debt I owe to Jesus, a debt of His great love."

Juliet served with distinction for 3 years until the mandatory retirement age of 40. The church in Swaziland was blessed by her leadership. She said, "I don't understand how God chooses people, but He chose me for the NYI work 'according to . . . his will'" (Eph. 1:5, KJV).

Later in 1966 Juliet was chosen to be ordained. At first she hesitated to accept. No woman had been ordained in the church in Swaziland prior to this time. The leaders said, "Why don't you pray about it?"

When she brought the matter before the Lord, He said, "No one will stand in your way; this is My finger upon your life." That promise was challenged when the presiding general superintendent expressed some reluctance to ordain her. Eventually, though, he was convinced that this was indeed the Lord's will.

At a highly emotional ordination service at Siteki in December 1966, Edward Kunene, Joseph Magagula, and Juliet Ndzimandze were ordained to the Christian ministry. When the general superintendent placed his hands on Juliet's head, I saw grown men cry. It was an electric moment in the history of the church in Africa.

Following this event, Juliet's preaching now became even more powerful. In May 1969 she preached at the young people's camp. She had never seen anything like it. From the first service to the last, dozens and dozens of young people bowed at the altar and found their way to Calvary for cleansing and sanctification. She said, "The Spirit was like that at Pentecost; the singing, praying, and shouting were anointed by power from on high. God was present in a tremendous way."

From that camp she went to Natal. "On Saturday the altar was lined with seekers, weeping, confessing, getting right with God. On Sunday morning we couldn't stop the service until 3 P.M. The Spirit from on high was present. Many hearts were uplifted. God was faithful to His promises."

By the conclusion of the second meeting Juliet said, "At first I felt God was calling me to Swazi youth work, but He told me plainly that He has chosen me; He will send me far unto the Gentiles. Now I am willing to go anywhere for Christ." The prophecy was about to be fulfilled. God was to be glorified, people converted, and the church established through His servant Juliet Ndzimandze.

In July Juliet preached at a women's retreat in Swaziland. "God has been good to me for allowing me to see such days of Pentecost in action," she said. "The fire from on high fell. . . . They shouted, sang, prayed, ran up and down, hugged, and marched around. God's presence was wonderful indeed. We pray that such a spirit might spread throughout all our churches."

As Juliet's ministry began to expand beyond the Bible college, some retired missionaries felt she could handle her evangelistic tours more efficiently if she did not have to depend on public transportation. So they bought her a used car. A fellow Bible college teacher helped her learn to drive, and Juliet successfully obtained her license. Many rejoiced in her new ability to go to churches where no bus or train traveled. However, on one of her early trips tragedy struck.

It was dusk as Juliet reached the top of the Site-ki mountain road. Just then a drunken woman coming from a "beer drink" staggered onto the highway. Juliet veered to the opposite side of the road to avoid hitting her, but at the very same moment the woman suddenly turned in the same direction, right into the oncoming car. She was killed instantly.

Juliet was gripped with grief. She was so overcome with remorse that she stayed in bed for days. Her appetite evaporated. Close friends stayed with her constantly in an attempt to assuage her sorrow.

The family of the woman sued Juliet. However, there were many witnesses who testified in court that there was nothing else Juliet could have done. In fact, they praised her for her attempt to avoid the woman and for her concern for the family. Juliet was completely exonerated by the judge, but she never drove again. For the next 25 years she endured many long bus trips and hours of strenuous walking because she felt that she should not drive.

Juliet never married, but it wasn't for lack of suitors. A certain bright and talented young man from another denomination had early tried to woo her. But Juliet was fiercely loyal to the Church of the Nazarene. She owed a great debt to the church. After all, her father had been its very first pastor in Swaziland. She wanted to be a servant of her own church. So in the end she turned down the pleadings of this young man. Today he is a leader of his denomination. In her later life, however, Juliet admitted that perhaps she had been a little narrow-minded in this decision.

A more spectacular overture for marriage came from none other than the king of Swaziland himself. The late King Sobhuza II began sending "friendly messages" to Juliet in early 1963, through a lady who acted as an intermediary. Those who were in the dormitory could tell that something was amiss. One said, "I would go to tell her that this lady had come to see her. I could tell by her face that something was wrong. She obviously did not want to talk with her. Sometimes she would say, 'I don't have time to talk with her.'"

There is an ancient custom in many parts of Africa that a ruler may unite a kingdom by intermarrying with significant subjects. Multiple wives were often taken, sometimes exceeding several dozen. Sometimes wives were taken not completely willingly. Emissaries of the ruler were sometimes dispatched to take a woman by mild force. Juliet knew these things.

The whole matter came to a head at a graduation ceremony at the Bible college. As some students were crossing the main road to the church, several recognized "all the king's men" in the cars parked on the road. During the ceremony someone whispered to Juliet as to what was up. In a tale of intrigue that befits a mystery novel, Juliet was hastily spirited out a side door and through a cornfield to a friend's house. There the dear friend locked Juliet in her room, pocketed the key, and went back to the church as though nothing had happened. The king's men never did find Juliet.

Missionaries and others knew if there had been one attempt to take Juliet, most likely there might be others. It was decided that the best thing to do was to get her out of the country. The very next day they drove her to the airport, where she flew to the central African nation of Malawi.

Juliet stayed in Malawi for a little less than a year. After things cooled down, she returned to Swaziland in mid-1964. For the rest of her life she would bear the burden and the honor of being "one who had refused the king." Later in life, after all was forgiven, she was able to preach and minister at the royal homestead and was on very good terms with members of the royal family.

Although many other suitors approached Juliet over the years, she chose to remain single. Her devotion was single-minded to the Lord. For this Juliet there would be no Romeo.

7

An Open Door

IN THE SEPTEMBER 1971 issue of *The Other Sheep,* Juliet tells of how God opened a new chapter in her life:

It was in the NYPS Convention of 1967 that God first spoke to me. Mfundisi Gailey talked about Moses carrying the cross of God in his youth. God spoke to me then, saying that He wanted me to carry the cross of youth work in Swaziland. For some time I thought that God meant to help in the leadership of NYPS in Swaziland. Later, in 1968, He made it clear that He wanted me to go out and hold youth meetings, to call our Swazi youth back to God.

God spoke to me again on New Year's Day, 1970. I remember those words as if He had spoken them this morning. On that day I was down in Zululand holding some meetings. He said, "Behold, I have set before thee an open door, and no man can shut it. Preach the word; be instant in season, out of season" [Rev. 3:8; 2 Tim. 4:2, both KJV]. From then on I felt that God would open many doors for me this year.

In the third week of March, I had four calls for revival meetings all at once in Natal, Acornhoek, Manzini, and Mshingishingini [(m)shin-gee-shin-GEE-nee]. I answered them all and said I was sorry I couldn't come because of my teaching job. On the very next day God called me very clearly. He spoke in English. I was on my knees in the chapel. He said, "Out and out for evangelistic work." That was on the 18th of March, 1970. Days come and go, but I can never forget what God said to me on that day. It was very hard for me to say yes there and then. I had to fast and pray for many hours. His hand dealt very gently. He said, "Are you afraid to take this step? Does it seem too sudden, too much like a leap into the dark? Does it involve too much? You think it is too great a risk?" It was hard to quit teaching because it had become a part of me.

It was there in that chapel late at night when I surrendered everything to God. I had to die once again to my own plans, aims, and ways. I said yes to God for life and for eternity. After I surrendered everything to Him, He visited me in a tremendous way. The heavens burst open and His glory came down. I was afraid that I was going to burst. God gave me many promises, but I can write only a few.

Deuteronomy 31:7-8: "Be strong and of a good courage: for thou must go with this people unto the land which the LORD hath sworn unto their fathers to give them; and thou shalt cause them to inherit it. And the LORD, he it is that doth go before thee; he will be with thee . . ." [KJV].

Acts 22:14-15: "The God of our fathers hath chosen thee, that thou shouldest know his will, and see that Just One, and shouldest hear the voice of his mouth. For thou shalt be his witness unto all men of what thou hast seen and heard" [KJV].

Though it was hard to tear myself away from the people who had loved me so much, I resigned in obedience to the will of God. From that day up to this there has been a live coal in my heart that has burnt day and night. From March up to this October, I have experienced a revival that I had never known before. Even if I don't live to see that great revival, I can say I have seen and experienced a great revival that has flooded my soul for many weeks and many months.*

Juliet submitted her resignation to the Bible college in 1970. Constantly before her was God's command: "See, I have placed before you an open door that no one can shut" (Rev. 3:8). Again many opposed the plan. Some said, "She's sick." Others complained, "How's she going to manage all the travel that will be involved?"

Juliet stepped out on faith and left the security of a regular salary. She didn't even know where she was going to live, and she knew that some opposed

---

*From Juliet Ndzimandze, "All I Am I Give to God," *The Other Sheep,* vol. 58, September 1971.

her, but she also knew that "we must obey God rather than men!" (Acts 5:29). Someone told her, "You're stepping out into darkness." She replied, "No! I am stepping out into the very arms of God. I have to walk by faith, not by sight." She completed her resignation and cleaned out her desk at the college in early December 1970.

Before 1971 began, letters had arrived from many different places, inviting her to speak. In addition to those from Swaziland, calls were coming from Durban, Pietermaritzburg, and the Transvaal, all in South Africa. God even opened doors in the great central city of Johannesburg, where millions lived. Juliet preached in youth revivals, camp meetings, other Bible colleges, and churches all around.

One of her first assignments after leaving the Bible college was to preach at the women's retreat at Endzingeni. The Spirit of God descended on the retreat in a remarkable way. The women were uplifted in spirit as never before and went home energized with a new vision for serving the Lord. Some have said it was the most blessed women's retreat ever held in Swaziland.

Then it was on to the Eastern Cape Young People's Convention in South Africa. To this day those who were there remember what happened. The service began late, but then God came in remarkable blessing. At the end, people just flocked to the altar. They prayed and prayed and had testimonies. Again the Spirit moved upon the crowd, and the altar filled a second time. Great victory ensued. Someone who was there said, "I thought perhaps

God had completed the work, but a third time the altar call was given, and people came and filled the altar." Another eyewitness exclaimed, "I had never seen anything of this nature before! God was there as one actually walking among us. People were praying all over the campground. God's presence was felt everywhere. In the night people were praying in the church. In the dormitories they were praying. Praise His name!"

One of the youth leaders in that service was Pat McKenzie, who is now a member of Parliament in the new South Africa. He led his community in closing the only bar in town. This and other effects of that single service will resound throughout eternity.

In 1978 the head of the Nazarene schools in Swaziland, after much prayer, asked Juliet to pray about holding revivals in the schools. Her response was, "Why did you wait so long? I've been expecting you to come, as the Lord has already laid this on my heart." God had told her, "I am sending you to the fields." And so she began.

Juliet would usually visit two schools a month, giving one week to each school. Since there were 40 schools and more than 12,000 students, it was a huge task. There would be as many as four services per day. In the morning there would be a service for the early grades, then another service for the older children. If there was a high school, that would require yet another service. Each evening there would be a meeting for the whole local church.

What services these were! Juliet's slowness of

speech allowed the children to follow her. They were attentive and came to the altar and wept. There were great visitations of the Holy Spirit. Perhaps remembering her own time alone at the altar as a teenager, Juliet felt she should counsel with each person who came forward, one-on-one.

By the afternoon, Juliet's energy was spent. In later life she said, "Humanly speaking, I felt I could not preach in the evening service, but God somehow gave me power. I was just amazed to receive new power. I meet adults all the time who say, 'I was saved in those services!' A few are ministers in the church." Missionary Ken Walker, the current field director, related, "As I accompanied her on these campaigns, I began to catch her vision."

Sandy Estey recalls the time that Juliet was to speak in services at the Teacher Training College in Swaziland. Sometime before the services were to begin, Juliet said that God had not given her a message. The week before, she still had none. She became quite concerned and wondered why He was not giving her a message. But she continued to trust Him. Then, on the very eve of the services, political turmoil spread throughout the nation. All schools, including the Teacher Training College, were closed. There were no services. Then she understood and trusted even more.

In 1980 God revisited Juliet and renewed her call through the words of Jer. 1:5: "Before I formed you in the womb I knew you, before you were born I set you apart; I appointed you as a prophet to the nations."

This baby who had been carried in her mother's womb to visit the dying Harmon Schmelzenbach was now, about a half century later, being sent by God far away to the nations. In 1984 Africa Regional Director Richard Zanner appointed Juliet as an evangelist for the whole continent of Africa. Calls were now coming from other nations, especially in Central and East Africa: Zambia, Zimbabwe, Malawi, Mozambique, and Kenya.

All over Africa, God's power was being evidenced through His servant. Her 1983 tour of Malawi was remarkable. People still remember her messages. Pauline Kamanga said, "She preached holiness and how to be filled with the Holy Spirit. She gave us a way to understand holiness." In another nation they reported, "God came upon us until we forgot there were other things on the program. The power of the Lord was felt in place after place."

Great blessing was gracing the African continent. But God had still other nations in mind—even beyond Africa.

8

Of Marriages and Money

THERE WAS A LONG LIST of "firsts" in Juliet Ndzimandze's life. She was the first full-time national teacher in the Nazarene Bible College, the first woman to be ordained in Swaziland, the first and only woman to be NYPS (NYI) president in Swaziland, and the first African elected to the Africa Literature Board.

Juliet was also the first woman marriage officer in Swaziland. In that country every minister desiring to conduct marriage ceremonies must be certified by first taking an extremely rigorous legal exam. Very few ministers pass this exam. But Juliet did—and in true Ndzimandze fashion, when she conducted a wedding, it was very special. Her first wedding after certification was conducted in the Ensingweni Church of the Nazarene. Those who were there will never forget it.

There is an ancient custom in Swaziland of putting red ocher on the face of the bride in order to solemnize a marriage. Red is symbolic, and Juliet was able to take just such an old piece of culture and bring Christian significance to it. Near the close of the ceremony, while the couple was kneeling, Juliet took a red streamer. She had the couple hold hands, and then

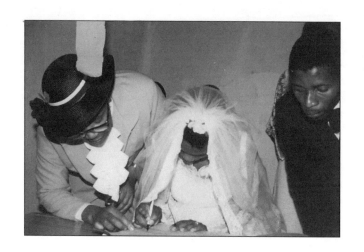

Officiating at her first marriage ceremony

she bound their hands together with the red cloth. She said, "This symbolizes the blood of Jesus, who died for this bride and groom on the Cross. The blood of Christ is actively uniting them in this marriage."

The whole church was moved. Something remarkable happened—the Holy Spirit swept across the room. Some people said "Amen." Some cried. Everyone was touched. The bride's mother and the pastor of the church cried. This first wedding was followed by many others. When Juliet conducted a wedding ceremony, people knew that it would be a very, very special occasion! Although she herself never married, Juliet learned how to marry others. She was also an effective marriage counselor. It was another part of her servanthood for God.

In 1968 the Swaziland District needed a new treasurer. People throughout the world know that the position of treasurer is one of the most delicate positions in the church. This post must be held by someone of absolute integrity and honesty. Naturally, the district turned to Juliet. Everyone knew that her character was without question.

Juliet didn't want the job, but they said, "We're in a difficult position. You must help us. All you need to do is just sign the checks." She finally agreed to help out temporarily.

Juliet ended up keeping the job of treasurer for 16 years. What a treasurer she was! As was her character, she learned to do whatever was needed. The district superintendent said, "She was just very, very good." Her reports were always precisely on time. If something was lost, she would pray.

When the World Mission accountant visited Africa, he said that of all of the people who came to the meeting of bookkeepers, Juliet asked the most intelligent questions. And for all of the 16 years, Juliet herself said, "I never lost a cent."

When the district budgeting system was introduced, Juliet was in the forefront. People are wary of change, and it was a difficult time. But she was tactful and precise, and above all, people trusted her implicitly.

Not only was she an efficient treasurer, but also she had a heart for people. Sometimes the assistant treasurer would see her write a check from her personal account to send to a pastor. He would say, "Why are you doing that?"

Juliet would reply, "The Lord has impressed me to send him money."

The assistant said, "Sure enough, later we would find out that the pastor was in need."

Juliet was loving and wise, but she could also be a disciplinarian. If a pastor brought in a jumbled report, she would put on a very stern face and reprimand him. But after he had left, she would laugh and laugh. Next time the report would be better! In later years Juliet was treasurer also of the Pension Fund for the district. She continued the Pension Fund job until 1992.

By this time Juliet was beginning to travel more widely as an evangelist. She was also having trouble with her eyes, since she would work long hours into the night on the treasurer's books. She begged to be allowed to resign, and each year in her report she would say, "The time for me to do this work is coming to an end." And each year the reply from the Swaziland District Advisory Board and District Assembly would be the same: "Ungahlala, hlala" ("Please stay on a little bit longer"). Even so, when the time finally came when she did leave, the district superintendent was so worried he said, "Ndzimandze is killing the work by leaving!"

The district superintendent did not have much confidence in Juliet's assistant treasurer, who took her place in 1984. Goodwin Chirwa was younger. The superintendent said to Juliet, "You will still be responsible for whatever happens." She continued to work with the 1985 report and then served as counselor to Chirwa right up until 1994.

Juliet was a good counselor. When Chirwa was feeling discouraged because of criticism and lack of acceptance, he would go to her. She would say to him, "Don't worry. The Lord is using this to make a man out of you. You need this to help you mature." Sure enough, today, more than 12 years after taking the job of treasurer, Chirwa is widely respected. The district superintendent says, "Chirwa does an excellent job." Juliet carefully prepared the way for this to happen.

Juliet also gave Chirwa some "life advice." When he and his wife would go to her, she would say, "When you go to town and see someone, say something good to them. Compliment them and encourage them." Juliet knew that the Chirwas, in encouraging others, would be encouraged themselves. This was yet another spin-off from the holy life lived by a servant of God named Juliet.

9

To All the World

THE SHINING, SLEEK 747 reached for the stars in the nighttime sky above Johannesburg. Juliet settled back in her seat. She thought about how God had led her in her ministry throughout Africa. Now, with some trepidation, she had accepted an invitation to preach in the British Isles. Anticipation, apprehension, and dismay mingled in her mind. Friends had warned her, "England will not be like Africa!" But she knew she could trust God, who had called her.

The next morning the big steel bird landed on the runway and taxied to the terminal at London's Heathrow Airport. There, loving Nazarenes received her with gracious hospitality. Over those next three months of 1974, she preached in churches in England, Scotland, and Ireland. There were adjustments, to be sure. She was preaching in English, which was a second language to her, and she wondered if the people really were understanding what she was saying.

In Africa people had flocked to the altar of prayer in great numbers. Here it was different. There seemed to be little overt demonstration.

However, the people were thoughtful, and God had promised her, "Some will be there who will pray." She did not feel that receptivity was high, however, and did not go overseas again for nine years.

In 1983 Juliet was invited by the Billy Graham Evangelistic Association to attend the Conference for Itinerant Evangelists in the Netherlands. This was a world conference of evangelists, and that aspect naturally appealed to one who was giving her life to evangelism. She applied again for her passport and prepared to go. Africa Regional Director Richard Zanner arranged for her to preach in Germany prior to the meeting. Once again she found herself at the international airport.

That evening she preached in the Frankfurt Church of the Nazarene. The next five services were held in state churches in different cities within Germany, with good crowds. "Many were attracted to see a Swazi woman preacher," she said. When she stood to speak, however, people realized that this person was, above all, the messenger of God: "That Sunday morning at Kremperheid, as the congregation was singing, I felt strangely warmed. The church was packed full, and God helped with the message. When the appeal was given, many came forward to dedicate themselves. God's mighty power was moving; what a wonderful time we had."

That evening in the Deutschland church, God gave Juliet liberty with the message, and once again the people responded. Some told her that that kind of service was a new experience for them. Juliet's response was characteristically simple: "To God be the glory."

In one of her last services in Germany there were many young people. Before she finished preaching, she felt God prompting her to open the altar. She was very dubious and told Him she didn't want to make a mistake. He said, "No, this is the time." At the conclusion of the message when she gave the invitation, so many people came forward that she asked them to stand so there would be room for others.

How she praised God for answering prayer! Now she was convinced that Westerners also would be responsive to the message. Before she left Swaziland, God had given her a passage of Scripture, Isa. 43:1-6. Of special significance for her were the words "I will give men in exchange for you, and people in exchange for your life" (v. 4).

Also included in the Isaiah passage were the words "When you pass through the waters, I will be with you. . . . When you walk through the fire, you will not be burned" (v. 2). Juliet did not realize how these verses would apply to her—until the evening of July 8. She looked into her pocketbook and discovered that the clutch bag containing her passport, tickets, and traveler's checks was missing. She realized that she had lost it at noon. It seemed that everything collapsed at that moment. What would she do? How would she make it to the Netherlands for the evangelists' conference? Her plans came crashing down.

In this crisis she learned that God's Church is a

global Church and that Christians really do help each other. The Church is not composed of just local units or national units, but there is a global interconnectedness of all of the parts of the family of God.

The corporate church, hearing of her loss, sprang into action. The German people prayed for her. Hans Zimmerman and his staff in Frankfurt labored to find travel documents for her. Richard Zanner worked around the clock to try to get a new passport and ticket. E. V. Dlamini, the immigration officer in Swaziland, and Mr. Pato at the Swaziland Embassy in Belgium worked hand in hand to procure the documents necessary to get a new passport. The answer came on July 12, when she was given British passport C653165 at Frankfurt. That afternoon she flew to Amsterdam, arriving there in time to hear Billy Graham give the opening address. Her response was "Praise His name!"

The Billy Graham Conference on Evangelism was a life-changing experience for Juliet. More than 4,000 evangelists from 134 countries of the world were gathered in Amsterdam. The messages by Dr. Graham touched her deeply. Speakers included Luis Palau, Ravi Zacharias, Festo Kivengere, G. Osei-Mersah, Chuck Colson, and many others. They represented many cultures from many points on the globe.

As with all of us, while Juliet learned about what God was doing in other parts of the world, her own life was enriched. After seeing pictures of the Graham crusades, she said, "My heart cries for such a crusade for Swaziland." But this vision included more than just Swaziland. As she listened to Billy Graham's opening message, "The Evangelist and a Torn World," her heart was challenged. The world would open to her message. She would become—in fact was already becoming—an evangelist to the world.

The Amsterdam Conference itself provided opportunity for her to minister in some state churches of the Netherlands. These services were arranged by the Billy Graham team. Some of these encounters were humorous. When people in one church were asked why they had come to the service, they replied, "We came to see a woman preach. We've never seen such a thing before."

In this same large church there was a high pulpit elevated some distance above the congregation. The stairway to it looked as though it went on forever. The bishop invited Juliet to ascend the stairs, but she looked up at the pulpit towering above her and quickly declined. "I'll just stand here on the platform," she said. At the close of the service, people throughout the congregation stood to be prayed for. Later the bishop confessed, "This is also my first time to hear a woman preach. But I hope that the power that we have sensed here today will continue and do its work in this place."

Of her European trip Juliet said, "I can never be the same. My life has been touched and refreshed, my commitment renewed, and my prayer life challenged. My goal is to reach the lost and win them to Christ." She was even more committed to being an evangelist to the world.

The next year Juliet was invited to give the main address at the General NWMS Convention in Anaheim, California, in 1985. She also preached in local stateside churches before and after the convention. The Americans loved her and seemed to be receptive, especially in places like South Carolina, as noted previously.

Juliet was invited to return to America in 1992 on the occasion of Louise Robinson Chapman's 100th birthday celebration. Even though her eyesight was failing due to diabetes, she felt that she should go. She wanted to represent Swaziland, where Dr. Chapman had served so well for two decades and where she had known Juliet as a young child.

Juliet needed a passport on very short notice, which looked like an impossibility. However, Nazarene laypersons like the private secretary to the king of Swaziland were able to exert some influence, and she received the passport in time. Someone else gave her $60 to help, and she was off to the airport. She actually arrived in Los Angeles three days early.

There is a time-honored custom in Swaziland to ask your closest, most intimate friends to help with your funeral preparations. It is a great honor to be asked to assist in this way. When Juliet arrived in California, Dr. Chapman requested Dr. Nina Gunter to take Juliet to the funeral home to view the previously selected casket. Juliet was surprised and pleased to be asked to do such a special thing.

The day of the great 100th birthday celebration

arrived. Many dignitaries were there, including a general superintendent and other leaders of the church. There were letters from the president of the United States and the governor of California. Many speeches were given that applauded the contributions of Dr. Chapman to the Nazarene World Mission Society, to the church at large, and to the community. Then it was time for the representative from Swaziland, where Dr. Chapman once had served.

Juliet rose from her seat and came forward to the microphone. In her hand she held a small Swaziland flag. Even though she felt self-conscious doing so, she began to wave the flag and say, "Mother Chapman, I hail you with a Swazi flag on your 100th birthday!" As she did so, Dr. Chapman began to cry. Great tears filled her eyes and began to spill down the face that had weathered a hundred years.

Juliet continued,

Swaziland loves you, our mother! You told the people about salvation. You told them about sanctification. You told them to "pay the whole price" for revival. They did that, revival came down, and it continued for years and spread out to the surrounding churches.

I remember when you came to Helehele on horseback and prayed with the workers. You prayed with my mother. I remember even now very clearly. Your face and my mother's face were both shining with glory from heaven. Heaven came down, and revival fires really burned.

May your mantle of faith, your mantle of

intercession, your mantle of doing battle—we pray that your mantle may fall on us.

Those who heard these words thought, "Yes indeed. The mantle of Dr. Chapman has fallen on this tall, regal person who is bringing this tribute."

Then, characteristically, Juliet ended on a humorous note:

> The private secretary to the king, who worked so hard to secure my passport in a very short time, has gone beyond that and bought me this outfit that I am wearing today, so that I may be presentable at Mother Chapman's celebration.

As she sat down amid laughter, Juliet said to Dr. Chapman, "They love you, Mother." It was a day to remember.

Although by this time Juliet was blind in one eye and her sight was failing in the other, she received invitations to speak in several churches on the West Coast on this trip. The nurse at Casa Robles became very concerned when she heard about her eye problem. She offered to help and took her to a Nazarene doctor. He arranged for specialists, who interrupted their schedules to do laser surgery on her eye. This resulted in some improvement. She spoke in several other churches and then returned to Swaziland.

Through the generosity of the same benefactor who paid for her eye surgery, Juliet was able to travel to the United States in order to attend the 1993 General Assembly in Indianapolis. She had received a special invitation to speak at the NWMS General Convention.

After General Assembly, Juliet traveled with retired missionary Edna Lochner to conduct revival services in 11 Midwestern churches. God blessed in those meetings. American Christians were helped and inspired as God's servant from Swaziland preached the Word. The Body of Christ who had sent missionaries to Swaziland were now receiving the blessing of a fresh touch from God through someone who had come from Swaziland. After the successful tour was completed, Juliet, as was typical of her, said, "I give all the praise back to God."

Juliet was very tired when she flew back to Swaziland. Once again she had been used of God to touch the American church. Once again He had fulfilled His promise in Isa. 43:4: "I will give men in exchange for you, and people in exchange for your life."

10

Back Home

BY THE EARLY 1990s Juliet's long battle with diabetes had forced her to reduce her speaking schedule. She had always been active in her local church, but now the opportunity for involvement increased.

Simon Mahlalela had joined Juliet's prayer chain years before, and the two had become good friends. When Juliet's home church, Sharpe Memorial Church of the Nazarene in Manzini, called Rev. Mahlalela as pastor, there was joy in her heart. They began to form the nucleus of a leadership team for the large, growing, urban church. Pastor Mahlalela declares, "She was my director in the church. She was like my mother, my father, my grandfather, and my grandmother all rolled into one."

When the committee began to talk about the much-needed building program in 1990, Juliet began to pray and fast. Money was raised to complete part of the building, and one wing was put up. The money was gone, but the building was not complete. The church borrowed E30,000 (U.S.$8,000) from the bank. They went back and borrowed

E40,000. Then they borrowed another E30,000. The money was gone, but the building wasn't complete. One board member said: "How are we going to repay all of this debt?" Juliet replied, "This is not our church—this is God's church. Let's bring what we can." Miraculously the debt was paid.

Then the church board ordered furniture for the new offices. When the pastor saw his desk chair, it looked to him like a chair "fit for a king," and he felt very uncomfortable using it. He considered it to be too elegant for a pastor and confided his feelings to Juliet. She replied in typical Ndzimandze fashion, "Have you prayed over this?" She called another member of the prayer chain and had the pastor kneel by the new chair as they prayed for him. From then on he had no problem in using the chair.

Later the church needed a new roof. The estimated cost was E55,000 (U.S.$13,000). The pastor took the need to Juliet. She said, "Oh, that's no problem. We'll report it to God. He has all power." Plans were also made for a new parsonage for 1997. Juliet said, "Yes, we'll do it, and we'll finish it too." In one of her last letters to us, Juliet wrote in feeble handwriting, "A month ago our joy at Sharpe Memorial Church was complete when we wiped off our debt at the bank for our new building. Sharpe has done well to finish in four years time a building that has cost more than E500,000. We have a praying pastor, committee, and church members."

Juliet's ability to inspire people to give themselves to prayer was matched by her ability to inspire people to give of their substance. In 1994 when she heard that the Bible college was in financial need, she said to the church, "We must raise money for the Bible college." Immediately the congregation raised over E3,000.

When the district needed a car for the district superintendent, they asked her to raise the money. The pledges flowed in. It was uncanny. Part of it was her absolute transparency. People trusted her. The rest of it was her total dependence on God. Everything she did was permeated by prayer.

Juliet's reputation had now gone beyond the Church of the Nazarene. Government officials were seeking her advice and prayers. In 1995 the prime minister of Swaziland asked Juliet and three other persons to come to his residence to pray for the nation. It was an open question as to whether she would be well enough to go.

The prime minister had heard that she was ill, so he requested the others to accompany her and walk on either side, taking a hand to support her. On the given day, this little group of earnest Christians drove to the capital and entered the prime minister's residence. What ensued next was remarkable. There in that home they had a great prayer service for the nation. God was helping His servant to be a herald of the importance of prayer. She had a vision that great revival would come to Swaziland if people would humble themselves and pray.

A few months later Juliet entered the hospital

again. This time it was very serious. She had a stroke and nearly died. One side of her body was immobilized, and her hospital stay stretched to three months. Near the end of this stay the regional directors and other church leaders from around the world had a conference in Africa, and they decided to travel by bus to Swaziland.

The bus deposited them in front of the hospital on Sunday morning, November 19, 1995. In small groups they came to her hospital room. By this time Juliet had recovered much of the use of her arm and, along with it, her humor. In her usual feisty way she reported, "My doctor said, 'Can you use this hand?' So I just reached up and biffed him with it!" Everyone was amused.

The author had the privilege of being in the room with her for the full hour as the visitors came and went. Louie Bustle, director of World Mission Division, expressed concern and prayer on behalf of the entire church. Juliet's response and her expression of gratitude for the prayers of global Nazarenes were videotaped: "[I represent] the answer to Nazarene prayers from around the world. . . . I give God the glory. . . . The doctors never thought I would walk again, but God has brought me out of bed, and I can walk a few steps. All of this is to the glory of God! He answers prayers in a wonderful way!"

The very next day, Juliet was discharged from the hospital. She was able to return to the miracle house on Dlamini Street, and she thanked God for the privilege. She said, "God has been good to me

Thanking the Church of the Nazarene from her hospital room in November 1995.

through many temptations, problems, and difficult family matters. But He has helped me through them all."

Of the five Ndzimandze siblings who had reached adulthood, the only other one living was Clarence. But she was encouraged about the future. She loved to repeat the verse: "In all these things we are more than conquerors through him who loved us" (Rom. 8:37).

11

Celebration

FOR NEARLY SIX MORE MONTHS Juliet was able to live in the miracle house and continue her ministry of prayer. Friends surrounded her to reciprocate some of the love that had flowed through her life to others. She began to say, "I want to go home. Now I am ready to go."

Out of concern for Juliet's health, someone was always with her. The local church hired someone to bathe and feed her. In typical fashion she began to joke, "I am ready to go. But I can't die, because people are praying that I will live. We need to reeducate these people and teach them how to pray so I can die!"

Juliet's lifelong friend (and elementary school teacher) Gloria Dlamini went to visit her every day, and she tried to get her whatever she asked for. If she missed a day, Juliet would say in a jocular vein, "Where have you been?"

Ellen Sibandze, another close friend of many years, came from Siteki once a month. When she arrived in April, Juliet said, "Where have you been? Don't you know I don't have long to live?" It was on this visit that she shared her plans that the funeral service would be one of joy and gratitude and

Ellen Sibandze, dressed in white for the funeral celebration.

not mourning. She didn't want people to dress in black mourning clothes. She said to Ellen, "You must wear white. I want it to be like a wedding."

On Sunday morning, April 28, 1996, Juliet was in church. Kind hands helped and lifted her as she slowly walked to and from the car. Later that day a prayer group met at her house as usual. On Thursday morning, May 2, she awoke feeling very ill and had to be rehospitalized. Word was sent throughout Swaziland. Over the next two days faithful friends circulated in and out of Room 7 at Raleigh Fitkin Memorial Hospital.

Early on Saturday morning, May 4, Associate Pastor Michael Themba went to see Juliet. After praying with her, he sensed that she was becoming weaker and called the nurse, who came at once. Phyllis Hynd also came. Juliet apparently sensed the gravity of the moment and said, "Pray! Pray!" Mrs. Hynd grasped one hand, and Rev. Themba the other. They prayed for several minutes, and when they looked down, she had stopped breathing. She had gone to be with Him whom she loved so much. She had died while praying. She was a woman of prayer, and she died as she lived.

Sometime in 1995 Juliet had written down complete plans for her funeral. She had put all of the plans in an envelope with the pastor's name on it and stored it. Her faithful Christian niece Miriam found it after her death and gave it to the pastor. Juliet had said to her friend Gloria, "I want my service to be a service of singing and rejoicing, not a funeral." When the pastor opened the envelope, he found the blueprint for such a service—right down to the songs to be sung. He and other friends carried out her directions.

Juliet's funeral was one of the most unusual ever held in Swaziland. The night before the funeral, friends gathered in the church. They went to pray and share together. It was a blessed time of remembering Juliet and recommitting their own lives to God.

The prayer chain members came to this gathering, and Juliet's friend Ellen reminded them that Juliet's place was now vacant. The chain was broken, so the invitation was made. "If someone would like to fill Juliet's place in the chain, that one could come forward. Who would fill the gap?" Amazingly, more than a dozen people rose and came forward and volunteered. Then, as one eye-witness said, "The heavens opened up, and God was with each of us until midnight, when we broke up."

Saturday, May 11, 1996, dawned as a clear, sunny day. More than 1,000 people crowded into the church for Juliet Ndzimandze's memorial service. People came from as far as 300 miles away. People from all stations and walks of life were there—people who had been touched by the divine imperative that was operative in Juliet's life.

Enoch Litswele was there. He said, "Rev. Ndzimandze came to Arthurseat in 1952. She sang at the camp meeting. I was helped to receive my call through her song." Today he is principal of the Nazarene Theological College in South Africa.

Petrus Pato was there. After a distinguished career as a college principal and a district superintendent, he is now teaching at the Nazarene Bible College in Malawi. Rev. Pato said, "Everything Juliet did was remarkable. When she was local NYPS president, she was excellent; when she was district NYPS president, it was beautiful; when she was district treasurer, she did it very well; when she was a Bible college teacher, she excelled; when she was an evangelist, she was very successful."

Speaker after speaker extolled her life—district superintendents, former pastors, educators. As she wished, the service was more a celebration of victory than a funeral. Ellen Sibandze was there, dressed in pure white: a white dress, a white sweater, a white hat. She spoke about the prayer chain. One of Juliet's last requests was to "keep the prayer chain going."

Juliet's longtime pastor at Siteki, Rev. C. Mnisi, conducted the graveside service. Then came the surprise announcement from her current pastor, Rev. Mahlalela. In her "funeral envelope" Juliet had left specific instructions, together with the funds, to provide a feast for everyone attending her funeral. She had even donated a cow for the occasion. As usual, she had thought of everything and had been able to pull it off as a total surprise and in a very good-humored way. People sat down to eat and rejoice. Although there had been no Romeo for this Juliet, she would be a part of His Church—the Bride of Christ—forever.

The earthly life of Juliet Kayise Ndzimandze is completed, but the lengthening shadow of her life continues in the lives she touched, literally around the world. Her name was Kayise, "daughter of her father"; but it was Rev. Samuel Dlamini, former student and now district superintendent of the Swaziland South District, who at the funeral gave her a new name. He said, "She is Twalizizwe, 'one who carried a burden for the nations.'" His spoken word is a fitting epitaph for one who was indeed an evangelist to the world.